GW00771720

The beauty of CANTERBURY

Photographs by Graeme Matthews

Published by Photoimage
Blenheim
New Zealand
Phone/Fax: +64 3 570 5655
Email: g.matthews@clear.net.nz
www.graemematthews.co.nz

Printed in China

Designed by Go Ahead Graphics, Christchurch

ISBN 978-0-9876554-8-6

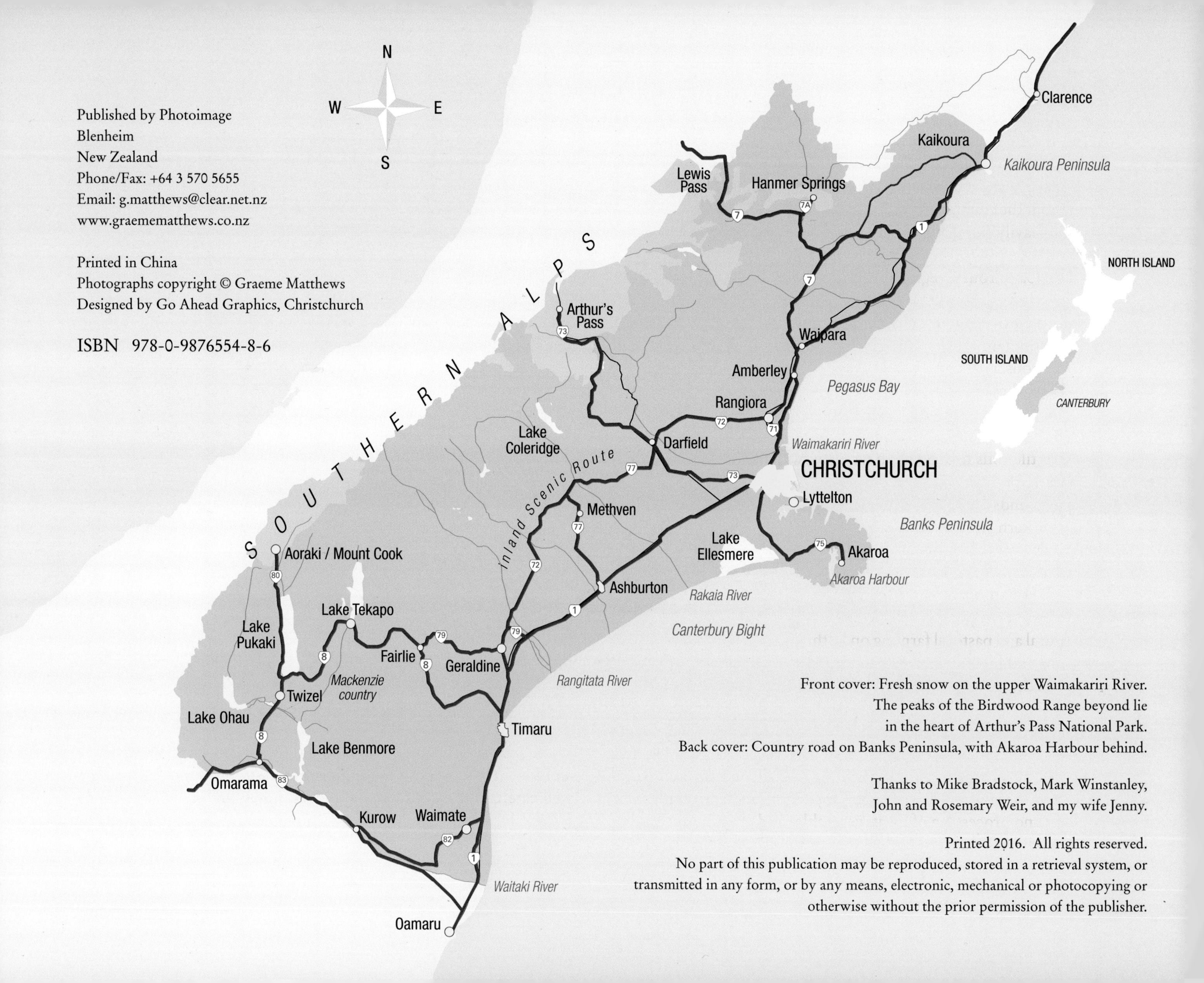

Front cover: Fresh snow on the upper Waimakariri River.
The peaks of the Birdwood Range beyond lie
in the heart of Arthur's Pass National Park.
Back cover: Country road on Banks Peninsula, with Akaroa Harbour behind.

Thanks to Mike Bradstock, Mark Winstanley,
John and Rosemary Weir, and my wife Jenny.

Printed 2016.

An introduction to Canterbury

About the 13th century, New Zealand (Aotearoa) was the last place in the world to be settled by humans as Polynesian ancestors of the Maori people arrived from the Pacific Islands. They quickly spread throughout the country but most of Otautahi, the Canterbury region, was not heavily populated when the explorer James Cook arrived in 1769.

The Canterbury region includes much of the South Island's east coast and the Southern Alps to the west. The Canterbury Plains were formed over the past 1.5 million years as vast glaciers carved out the mountain valleys, spreading rocks and gravel into broad fans up to a thousand metres thick near the coast. The big rivers that flow across these plains are "braided" – wide gravel beds with many water channels that shift after every flood of snowmelt or heavy rain. A legacy of this landscape is a fine supply of artesian water and, in places, fertile soils formed from wind-blown silt.

The Alps intercept the dominant westerly winds so that most rain falls on the western side, outside the region, and the dry northwest wind that results creates interesting cloud formations, particularly in summer. Mostly the climate is cool temperate and suitable for agricultural and pastoral farming on both the plains and high country backed by high mountains.

Since the mid-19th century British and European settler farmers have greatly changed the face of the land and today dairy, sheep, deer and beef farming, cropping and horticulture are widespread. Crops include seeds for export as well as stock feed and vegetables, and there are extensive areas of timber trees, especially radiata pine. Rural towns and the city of Christchurch support this industry, with wool handling and processing of meat, vegetables and grain, seed cleaning and sawmilling. Primary industry has always been the backbone of the regional economy, though fortunes have fluctuated greatly. Large high-country farms known as sheep stations specialise in producing fine wool from Merino sheep that wander high in the mountains during summer before being mustered in autumn and kept over winter on lower, flatter country during the breeding season and spring. Some farms have diversified into tourism and operate jet-boat trips, guided hunting and fishing, farm tours and farm stays.

Irrigation has played a crucial role in the development of lowland (and increasingly upland) farming, reducing the impact of droughts. Irrigation also enables more soil types to be successfully farmed, and has helped to diversify agriculture, especially dairying and cropping. Large herds of cows, fields of grain and grape plantings for winemaking are widespread. However, in recent years pressure on water resources has become a major environmental issue.

Tourism is an important feature of the Canterbury economy, with the mountains a particular drawcard, as seen in the famous Lord of the Rings movies. Overseas tourists and New Zealanders alike enjoy the clear skies and vast open spaces, which offer skiing, backpacking and sightseeing. There are two national parks in Canterbury (Aoraki / Mt Cook and Arthur's Pass) and many other large reserves of southern beech forest and alpine landscape. The glaciers and highest mountains such as Aoraki /Mt Cook are particular tourist attractions. As well as many native birds such as the unique alpine parrot (the kea), there are introduced game animals including red deer, fallow deer, chamois and Himalayan tahr.

Canterbury people are noted for their sense of community pride and for warmly welcoming overseas tourists, who find their needs well catered for by backpacker lodges, hotels and motels, excellent restaurants and other facilities. Campervans are a popular way of touring. "Cantabrians" also take pride in their region's "clean and green" image.

Above: Fur seals at Kaikoura. Along with dolphins and whales, these marine mammals are a popular tourist attraction and can easily be seen from many vantage points on State Highway 1 along the coast.
Opposite: Sunset on the pebble beach north of Kaikoura township. The sea here drops off to phenomenal depths, with the continental shelf in places extending only a few kilometres offshore.

Limestone platforms form wide reefs along the coast of the Kaikoura Peninsula.
The name Kaikoura means 'to eat crayfish' (rock lobster) and reflects the abundance of fisheries resources in the area.

An aerial view of the Kaikoura Peninsula.

Above: Dusky dolphin cavorting off Oaro, south of Kaikoura. These tame and playful dolphins are very common along the coast.

Opposite: Giant Sperm whale diving off Kaikoura. Whale-watching has become Kaikoura's most important tourist attraction and the great mammals can be observed from boats, aircraft and sometimes from the shore.

Exotic trees on farmland near Cheviot, North Canterbury.

St Anne's lagoon, in Cheviot Hills Reserve a few kilometres north of Cheviot. This 40-hectare reserve features some of the nation's largest specimens of exotic trees, some of which were planted as early as the 1850s. This was originally the home of one of Canterbury's earliest runholders, William "Ready Money" Robinson, so-named because of his enormous wealth that enabled him to pay cash for the 84,000-acre Cheviot Hills estate.

Above: 'The Cathedral', Gore Bay, North Canterbury, is a spectacular example of 'badlands' erosion.

Opposite: Sheep in early morning mist, North Canterbury. While sheep farming was the original foundation of New Zealand's pastoral economy, the fluctuating fortunes of meat and wool have seen the national flock dwindle over the years.

Above: Motunau Beach, North Canterbury, with a fishing boat returning at dusk. This tidal river mouth provides a safe haven for small craft and supports a valuable export rock lobster fishery.
Opposite: The same beach at low tide. Motunau Island in the distance is a wildlife sanctuary and home to many sea birds.

Early-morning mist burns off, ushering in a fine day on a minor road near Greta Valley, North Canterbury.

A herd of mixed cattle breeds, North Canterbury.

Above: Waipara River, in the Waipara Valley north of Christchurch – a well-known wine-growing district.

Opposite: Pastoral scene near Greta Valley as the last morning mist dissipates. The hills behind are clad with woodlots of Monterey pine (*Pinus radiata*), a timber tree that grows exceptionally well throughout New Zealand.

A disturbed northwest sky over the Waipara riverbed.
Northwesterly weather provides the heat that makes this area so successful at ripening grapes.

Vineyards near Waipara. The eastern hills behind provide shelter from the cool easterly winds that frequently blow in summer, creating a unique microclimate for the sauvignon blanc and pinot noir grapes that yield award-winning wines.

Nets over ripening grapes in midsummer. Birds need to be kept off the fruit at this crucial time and a variety of noise-making devices are also used to repel them.

Autumn colours, Waipara. The lean, stony soil and limestone basement rock create an ideal terroir for a distinctive local wine style.

Steam locomotive A428 was built in 1909 for the passenger express services in the North Island.
It is now the only working example of its class and operates periodically on the Weka Pass vintage railway between Waipara and Waikari.

A young driver on the Weka Pass to Waikari excursion service.
The enthusiasm for steam is not confined to the elderly in New Zealand.

Frog Rock, a striking natural limestone landmark alongside the Weka Pass Railway and State Highway 7, north of Waipara.

Maori rock art under limestone rock overhangs near Waikari.
These figures date from the early phase of human settlement of Aotearoa/New Zealand, probably not long after AD 1200.

Above: Boby Stream, North Canterbury, cuts a deep gorge through the soft limestone hills.

Opposite: Horse trekking on the rolling limestone hills near Waikari.

Above: Purple hues cover a North Canterbury field.

Opposite: Clearing mist, North Canterbury. Shelter belts of pine trees provide valuable protection against the drying northwest winds.

Horses on a stud farm. Canterbury is an important centre for the bloodstock industry and many internationally famous racehorses, both trotters and gallopers, have come from here.

Rainbow over Marble Point, in the Waiau Valley near Hanmer.
This area has recently been largely converted to irrigated dairy farming and vineyards.

Waiau River, near Hanmer Springs, after a heavy northwest rainfall in its headwaters. Much less rain falls this far to the east. The field in the midground is planted in lucerne (alfalfa), an increasingly popular forage crop in dryland farming areas.

The Waiau River bridge near Hanmer, location of the ‘Thrillseekers’ tourist operation that offers a 35-metre bungy jump, jet-boat rides and offroad quad biking.

Above: Hot springs are the main year-round tourist attraction of Hanmer, which also features many holiday homes belonging to Christchurch and Canterbury residents.

Opposite: The main road of Hanmer township features a long median strip of mature trees.

Above: Scullers training on the Kaiapoi River. The town of Kaiapoi was once a major Canterbury port and home to rural industry including wool processing and flaxmilling. Today it is a nearby satellite town of the city of Christchurch.

Opposite: A beech tree overhangs Lake Christabel, a small lake in the Victoria Forest Park, near Lewis Pass.

Above: The Christchurch trams drive around a circuit in the central city and are popular with tourists and locals alike.

Opposite: Cathedral Square, Christchurch. Despite the severe earthquakes of 2010 and 2011, the city is making a rapid recovery. Art galleries, theatres and museums are being rebuilt, repaired and re-opened and a spirit of optimism prevails.

Another Project
Managed by:
pace
PROJECT MANAGEMENT
30

The pier on the coast at New Brighton, Christchurch, easily reached by bus or a 15-minute drive from the central city.
The sandy beach is popular with walkers, swimmers, surfers and kitesurfers.

A black-backed or Dominican gull on the New Brighton pier.
One of the more common sea birds around New Zealand's coasts and rivers.

Canterbury Museum, next to the Botanic Gardens in central Christchurch, was opened in 1870.
Built in the Gothic Revival style like many early public buildings, it survived the earthquakes well and has been re-opened to the public.
Its displays include early Maori artefacts, Chinese antiquities and an outstanding polar history collection.

The Peacock Fountain, in the Christchurch Botanic Gardens.
Built in 1911, it was later disassembled and kept in storage for many years before being recommissioned in 1996.

Above: A schoolboy rugby team after a hard-fought match in Hagley Park. This 165-ha public space in central Christchurch is one of the world's largest city parks, and boasts a golf course, cricket oval, tennis and netball courts and many open public spaces.

Opposite: A cycling, walking and running track borders Hagley Park. The park is also a venue for concerts and other public events.

Cyclists on a track lined with cherry trees, Hagley Park.

New Regent Street, central Christchurch, features Art Deco architecture, boutique shops, restaurants and cafés.

Above: Punting on the tree-lined Avon River from the boatsheds on Antigua Street.
This excursion takes passengers upstream between Hagley Park and the Botanic Gardens.

Opposite: Canoes and rowing boats can also be rented at the Antigua Street boatsheds.

Canoeists and Canada geese share the tidal waterway of the Avon-Heathcote Estuary, Christchurch.

Lyttelton is the main port of Canterbury, nestled in a harbour at the north end of Banks Peninsula and connected to Christchurch by road and rail tunnels. As well as handling import and export cargoes it is an important deepwater fishing port with a dry dock and engineering services. It is also a fashionable residential town with a character of its own.

Governors Bay jetty at the head of Lyttelton Harbour. This area was once slated to become the city of Christchurch until the founding fathers concluded there was insufficient land and decided instead to build across the hills to the north. Today it is a quiet bushy residential area, twenty minutes' drive from the city.

Harness racing at Motukarara on a Sunday afternoon. Motukarara, on the Christchurch–Akaroa road, hosts racing events in a rural setting, and draws crowds from the city.

JOHN DEERE
6830

Above: Akaroa Harbour on Banks Peninsula.
Opposite: Tractor hauling giant discs to till a paddock on an arable farm, Southbridge, prior to sowing spring crops.
Crops grown in the area include grain, potatoes and seed crops, as well as winter forage for stock. Canterbury produces 80 percent of the nation's grain and seed crops, and half the world's carrots and radishes are grown from New Zealand seeds.

Akaroa Harbour, on Banks Peninsula. The first European settlement in this area was by the French in 1840 after Jean Langlois, a whaler, purchased 30,000 acres of land in 1838. However, in the meantime the Treaty of Waitangi, signed by Maori and English parties, pre-empted this attempt at establishing French sovereignty. Akaroa Harbour today is a popular tourist destination and frequently visited by cruise ships. A marine reserve protects endangered wildlife including the unique Hector's dolphins.

Pohutukawa blossoms, Akaroa. Also known as the New Zealand Christmas tree as it flowers heavily in December, this is an iconic maritime tree widely cultivated outside its natural range.

Akaroa Harbour
Nature Cruises
Swimming
With Dolphins
Gift Shop and Booking Office
CRUISES

Above: La Belle Villa, Akaroa township.
Apart from French street names and house names there is little today to show this town's origins.

Opposite: Akaroa wharf is the base for the dolphin-spotting and 'swim-with-the-dolphins' operations, popular with tourists.

Akaroa Harbour and township at sunset, with a cruise ship beyond.
The hill on the skyline centre left is known by a French name, Mount Bossu (Hunchback).

White-fronted tern, (*Sterna striata*), Banks Peninsula.

Oxford, a typical small inland Canterbury town that services the rural industries.

Snow on the Christchurch to West Coast road. This very scenic route (State Highway 73) passes over plains, through mountain passes and beech forest before leaving Canterbury and descending to the West Coast.

Above: Lake Pearson under a northwest sky in winter.
One of the many high-country lakes along State Highway 73, bordered by tussock grasslands.
Opposite: The Waimakariri River in winter, with the braided pattern of riverbed and flood channels clearly etched by a fresh fall of snow.
Clouds in the distance shroud the mountains of the main divide.

The rugged landscape of the Waimakariri River headwaters, in the heart of Arthur's Pass National Park.
A young, dramatic and rapidly eroding landscape constantly shaped by earthquakes, heavy rain and snow.

Castle Hill Station, with curious natural limestone rock formations, lies on State Highway 73, west of Christchurch.
Behind is the Porters ski field, one of the most popular and easily accessible ski fields in the region.

Above: A short distance west of the main divide near Arthur's Pass, the highway descends steeply along the Otira Viaduct towards the west coast. The 440-metre, four-span viaduct is just part of a long, steep descent over unstable, earthquake-prone land.

Opposite: The Punchbowl Falls (131 metres) lie a short walk through subalpine forest from Arthur's Pass village.

Fresh snow on foothills alongside State Highway 73. Most of this land is in native tussock grasses and shrubs.
Once part of Canterbury's high-country sheep stations, much of the hilly land has recently been transferred to the conservation estate following high-country tenure review.

This historic woolshed at Homebush near Darfield, was built in the 1850's, and is visible from the Inland Scenic Route.
It was built out of bricks made at the Homebush Pottery and Tile Works.
It is a magnificent legacy of pioneering rural life and is classified as an historic building.

Shelter belts and farmland immediately below the Rakaia River gorge, inland Canterbury.
A steep road along the ridge behind provides access to Mt Hutt skifield in winter.

Tussock grasses and hardy shrubs in the throat of the Rakaia Gorge. Very strong northwest winds that drive through this area carry quantities of dust and this forms valuable loess soils on the plains.

Jet-boat rides are popular on the scenic Rakaia River, which also boasts a good salmon fishery in autumn.

Above: Lake Coleridge, in a northern basin of the Rakaia Valley,
is one of numerous lakes formed behind giant moraines (rock dams) left after the last glaciation.
Opposite: A fresh autumn snowfall on tussock grasslands of the Southern Alps foothills.

Above: A forage crop of kale grown on the inland plains.
These crops, supplemented with hay or silage, provide essential fodder for stock during the harsh Canterbury winters.
Opposite: Lake Coleridge is located 35 kilometres to the northwest of Methven, and has a surface area of 47 km^2.
The Lake Coleridge Power Station is one of the country's earliest hydroelectric schemes, completed in 1914.

A giant leaping salmon greets visitors to the town of Rakaia, 60 km south of Christchurch.
Quinnat salmon in the Rakaia River sometimes grow as large as 20 kg and are eagerly sought by sport anglers.

Spring daffodils in the town of Ashburton, 90 km south of Christchurch on State Highway 1.
The major year-round climatic fluctuations of the South Island produce striking seasonal changes.

Above: Picnickers in the Ashburton Domain Park.
Most Canterbury towns have attractive, well-established parks and public lands that provide pleasant places for travellers to stop and rest.
Opposite: The lake in Ashburton Domain Park. Many species of waterfowl are common including mallard duck,
black swan, scaup, paradise duck, pukeko and Canada geese.

At Peel Forest Park Scenic Reserve, in the central Canterbury foothills, farmlands are backed with mature forest that suggests what the general landscape was like before human intervention. There are numerous short walks and an excellent camping ground.

Acland Falls, Peel Forest Park Scenic Reserve. This is an easy one-hour round trip walk, through native forest.

Above: Early morning light at Lake Camp, one of the Ashburton Lakes, located in a subalpine basin in the foothills of South Canterbury.
A popular venue for walking and fishing.
Opposite: Autumn muster on Hakatere Station, near the Ashburton Lakes.
The animals need to be brought down from their subalpine grazing grounds before winter snows begin to fall.

Right: The Maori Lakes are part of the group of waterways known as the Ashburton Lakes. Early Maori travellers gathered food from these lakes, as they made their way from one coast to the other. This locality is a nature reserve and is also popular for wilderness trout fishing.

Above: The broad, bleak landscape of the Hakatere Conservation Park, part of the Te Araroa Walkway. Hakatere is the Maori name of the Ashburton River, whose upper reaches flow through the park between the Rakaia and Rangitata Rivers.

The Sacred Heart Basilica, Timaru, is one of South Canterbury's most important historic buildings.
Designed by the architect Francis Petre and completed in 1911,
it features Roman and Byzantine styling and is a conspicuous feature of the Timaru skyline.

Blackett's lighthouse at Caroline Bay, Timaru, was built in 1878. It was controversially moved from its original site in 2010, to its new site on Benvenue Cliffs. It is no longer used as a navigation beacon.

The statue of Phar Lap at Phar Lap Raceway, Timaru. He was a champion throughbred racehorse in the late 1920's to early 1930's. Although he was trained and raced in Australia, he was foaled at Seadown, near Timaru in 1926, and is rightly regarded as a New Zealand icon. The life-size bronze statue at Timaru's Phar Lap Raceway was created by Joanne Sullivan-Gessler.

St Mary's Anglican Church, Timaru, was consecrated in 1866 and built largely after the style of the Christchurch Cathedral. It was extensively damaged in the September 2010 earthquake but re-opened in 2015.

Walkway at Caroline Bay, Timaru. A picturesque beach, it is one of few sheltered areas along the South Island's east coast, and very popular for recreation and public events including an annual summer carnival. The sand dunes have been extensively re-planted in recent years.

Chalmers Presbyterian Church, Timaru, was designed by J.S. Turnbull and consecrated in 1904.
In 1907 it was said to have hosted the first New Zealand wedding to which the bride was brought by motor car.
The church has now been decommissioned and is privately owned.

A northwest cloud formation over the Opuha River, South Canterbury.
The 'Nor'west arch' is a weather pattern common to the east coast of New Zealand's South Island. For this reason, it is also often referred to as the 'Canterbury arch'. It is shown in an apparent arch of high white cloud in an otherwise clear blue sky over the Southern Alps.

Rolling hills farmland near Geraldine, South Canterbury.

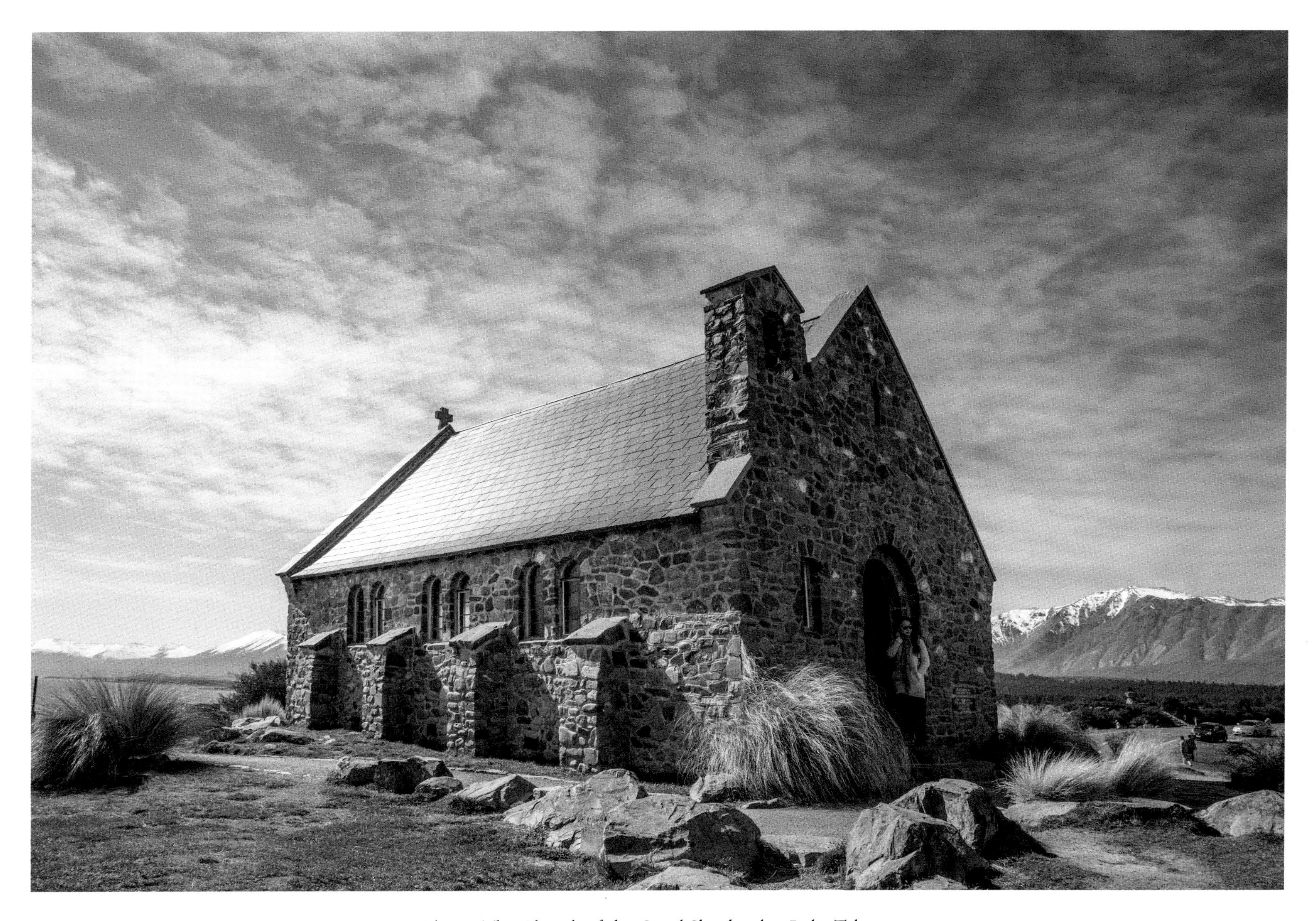

Above: The Church of the Good Shepherd at Lake Tekapo.
This interdenominational church was built from local stone in the 1930's and is a popular tourist attraction.
Opposite: Lake Tekapo, Mackenzie country, inland Canterbury.
Dense northwest cloud signifies rain in the head of the Godley Valley behind.

This statue of a sheepdog, near the church at Lake Tekapo, was erected in 1968 as a tribute to the countless generations of working dogs that have served New Zealand farmers. The first such dog to enter the Mackenzie country, in 1855, was 'Friday', belonging to the legendary sheep rustler James Mackenzie, after whom the high-country basin was named.

Lake Alexandrina, a crystal-clear spring-fed lake near the town of Tekapo, boasts a fishery for trophy rainbow and brown trout.

Above: Lake McGregor, in the Mackenzie country, in autumn colours and with the foothills of the Southern Alps beyond.

Opposite: Shafts of light passing through dust in strong northwest winds in the Two Thumb Range above Lake Tekapo.

Mackenzie country, with foothills shrouded in cloud.
Ten thousand years ago this entire subalpine basin was buried under a great sheet of glacial ice.

Russell lupins are a striking and colourful feature of roadsides and stream banks in the Mackenzie country.

A high-country runholder mustering with dogs in the Mackenzie country, inland Canterbury.

The braided Rakaia River. These enormous valleys were carved out by great glaciers during the last ice age and have since been partly filled with rock and gravel worn down from the mountains behind. This process is still continuing, with the mountains being pushed up slightly faster than they are eroded.

Above: Aoraki / Mt Cook at its best, seen from the south. It is still New Zealand's highest mountain, at 3724 metres, despite having lost 40 metres during a great rockslide in 1991.
Opposite: Early morning on Lake Pukaki. This view of Aoraki / Mt Cook (centre skyline) is one of the most popular scenic attractions in the whole of New Zealand.

Lake Pukaki in the Mackenzie country, with Aoraki / Mt Cook dominating the skyline far behind.
The lakewater colour is due to ground-up rock particles.

An aerial view showing the extent of the Tasman Glacier. Although still New Zealand's longest glacier, at more than 20 km, it is now shrinking by hundreds of metres each year, leaving a growing lake at its base.

Sunset over the Southern Alps.
Tapered orographic clouds signal high winds from the west, a characteristic Canterbury weather formation.

A mountain climber is dwarfed by a deep crevasse on the Tasman Glacier, Aoraki / Mt Cook National Park.

Above: River braids and snow form an elaborate pattern along the Tasman River.

Opposite: Morning cloud lifting off the Southern Alps – a fine day will follow.

Mountains of the upper Tasman Glacier in moonlight.

The upper Tasman Glacier and Hochstetter Dome behind.

Above: Malte Brun Range, on the eastern side of the Tasman Glacier.
These mountains all form part of Aoraki / Mt Cook National Park, popular with climbers, backpackers and sightseers.
Opposite: Hochstetter Dome (2823 metres), at the head of the Tasman Glacier.
One of the numerous high peaks on the main divide in Aoraki / Mt Cook National Park.

Part of the Malte Brun Range, in Aoraki / Mt Cook National Park.

The Pyramid (856m) and the surrounding area between Lake Ohau and Lake Pukaki, where several episodes of 'The Lord of the Rings' were filmed.

Autumn colours, Mackenzie country. This whole area is strewn with small lakes, ponds and waterways that provide shelter and scenery in every season.

Cyclists alongside the Ohau Canal, on the Alps 2 Ocean cycleway.
This popular cycling route passes from the Aoraki / Mt Cook village down the watershed of the great Waitaki River to meet the Pacific Ocean at Oamaru. The canal is part of an extensive hydro-electric scheme.

Above: Lake Ohau and the Ben Ohau Range foothills, Mackenzie country.
Canals joining the high country lakes feed a hydro-electric power scheme along the Waitaki River.

Opposite: Loch Cameron, near Twizel in the Mackenzie country.

Low morning cloud over Lake Benmore, in the Waitaki Valley.
Built behind the nation's largest earth dam, it receives water for hydro-electric generation
from the entire Mackenzie country watershed.